Life Lessons From Torn Socks

Howard Anthony Roach

ISBN: 9798663274845 (paperback)

Printed in the United States of America

Table of Contents

Dedication

This book is dedicated to my two super cool, amazing and wonderful daughters, Roni Imani and Danielle Abigail.

(My socks are safe, but the t-shirts are now in danger).

OMS! (Oh My Socks)

It was a Thursday morning and I was rushing to get out of the house. The morning traffic can be a nightmare and after having a really good night's rest, I was going to do everything in my power to avoid being caught in the horrendous long lines and with environmentally unfriendly emissions emanating from everything that has an engine. I remember moving almost at the speed of an Olympic athlete, doing the decathlon with only two things left to do in the event. I quickly opened the drawer, retrieved my socks, and ran to the living room to do the socks-shoes combo, then I would be out the door, crossing that imaginary finish line. Then it happened. As I slipped the sock on my left foot, I saw my five toes and heel, not covered but exposed. That would have been an OMG moment, but it was definitely an OMS (oh my socks) moment. How did this happen? It was my favorite pair of brownies. As I looked closer, I realized that the sock was neatly and evenly cut. Then it hit me. My daughters are with a dance company. I remember watching a performance and part of the costume was brown socks with toes and heels exposed. Mystery solved. Time was not waiting for me; I had to make a decision; to wear or not to wear was the question. You guessed it; I wore the torn sock to work. After all, who but me would know (unless my shoe fell off) that it was not road worthy.

I did not expect that my day would begin the way it did. But as I left home, I was reminded of what **Romans 8:28 says**, **"And we know that all things work together for good to those who love God, to those who are the called according to His purpose." (NKJV).** Sometimes what appears to be a distraction or delay, is actually an opportunity to learn, change and grow.

Very often we magnify simple things that could be overlooked or even ignored. Our focus and emotions become so engaged and enraged. We consume our time with what is ultimately unnecessary, missing out on a chance to exploit opportunities that sometimes come only once in our lifetime.

LESSON NO. 1

Sometimes what appears to be a distraction or delay, is actually an opportunity to learn, change and grow. Very often we magnify simple things that could be overlooked or even ignored.

The Bigger Picture

I had a task; I had a mission to complete that day. I was a teacher of Guidance at an all-girls high school in Kingston. I loved going to my classes, interacting with my students, learning from them, even as I tried to motivate them to become what I coined their "better-best" selves.

Can you imagine me, calling in to the principal with tears and saying, "I'm so sorry, I can't come in today. I am traumatized! My children destroyed my favorite pair of brown socks."

Life is not perfect and, yes, things can and will happen that affect us deeply, like being betrayed by someone in whom we had confidence, making bad choices and decisions that even today the ripple effects still haunt us.

Perhaps you can identify with the words of **Psalm 42:5, "Why are you cast down, O my soul? And**

why are you disquieted within me? Hope in God, for I shall yet praise Him for the help of His countenance." (NKJV).

Regardless of our challenges, God has a purpose for our lives and that means, by extension, everything that happens to us, whether great or small, is significant. There are no accidents; there is no coincidence. It is all part of the bigger picture.

I like having eggs, as I am sure you do too. However, we cannot enjoy the egg without the shell being broken. Quite often the interruptions we face in our daily lives serve to break us from our routine so that we can tap into the things that ordinarily we would ignore or never recognize that we possess inside. There are good and even great things we have yet to discover about ourselves, and it is never too late.

As I ran over in my mind what happened in the morning, I thought, "Wow! Who would have thought that a mutilated sock could offer any life lesson?" Imagine for a minute some of the things that have taken place in your life, maybe this very day. What was God trying to say to you or teach you? I was now more excited than ever to see my students and share my strange story with them. Granted, these were high school girls who lived in a "perfect image" crazed society, so this was either going to be one of my most interesting classes or most embarrassing. But I was ready.

LESSON NO. 2

Regardless of our challenges, God has a purpose for our lives and that means, by extension, everything that happens to us, whether great or small, is significant.

Truth Destroys Fear And Shame

I arrived at school and suddenly I became a little bit more conscious that I was not "all together." This possible scenario immediately came to my mind. *I'm walking in front of a group of students, someone accidentally steps on the heel, shoe falls off, toes exposed, laughter and embarrassment.* If that were to happen, I am sure I would be forever greeted with: Good morning, Mr. Toes instead of Mr. Roach. That kind of shame I could well do without, so I avoided any crowd and walked by myself straight to my classroom.

There are people who live every day in fear that someone might discover things from their past and, if that happened, the shame and humiliation would be too much to bear. Fear and shame have the potential to cripple the bravest among us. Truth, however, is liberating. Sometimes we must make ourselves vulnerable, even to the worst of critics as, ultimately, our desire is to get past anything that hinders our personal growth and development. Interestingly, the topic for class that morning was: "Facing Your fears." The best way I believe you can overcome your fear(s) is to expose and confront them. So right after we did the usual greetings, I asked the students to sit in a circle then class would begin.

I said, "Ladies, today we will be looking at the topic: 'Facing Our Fears,' but first I have to face my own."

I now had a captive audience. I could tell by the look on their faces and their comments that they thought I was going to say I was afraid of some crawling thing or being in the dark. They were in for a surprise. Without warning, I whipped off my shoes and, bam; torn socks, toes and heel exposed. The classroom erupted in laughter. Eventually the laughter subsided and my students asked me why did I wear that torn sock. Some students even said I was "brave" and wondered if I was not worried what people would say. After giving them a synopsis of what happened, we started to discuss the topic for the morning. At the end of the hour, the girls did not want to leave, even though it was time for lunch. The discussion about their personal fears, dealing with and getting past them was at times heartbreaking, very enlightening and transformational. The truth is, facing our fears is not something easy, but it is so important that we do it.

I remember seeing this quote: "Being brave isn't the absence of fear. Being brave is having that fear, but finding a way through it."[1]

Imagine for a few minutes just how your life could be free from the debilitating effects of fear. The possibilities of a more fulfilled life will be yours for the taking. King David, as powerful as he was, had fears too. But listen to how he dealt with those fears.

"I prayed to the Lord, and he answered me. He freed me from all my fears." Psalm 34: 4 – (NLT).

Has fear kept you as its prisoner? If the answer is yes, perhaps this is the moment when you will decide no more, and, with God's grace and power, confront, overcome and begin to live the life you were destined to have.

---

[1] Bear Grylls

LESSON NO. 3

Fear and shame have the potential to cripple the bravest amongst us. Truth, however, is liberating.

Laugh At Yourself

At times, life can be hard and filled with surprises that are not always as pleasant as we would like them to be. Some of the challenges we face, however, are not as big as we make them out to be. If I use my mind to magnify an ant to the size of an elephant, the reality is, the ant is still as small as it ever was. We often make our fears and other challenges more than they really are and, before we know it, we become stressed out and unhappy.

I could have chosen to be upset with my children. Instead, in the end, I became a sort of class clown for the day as my students and I laughed because that was what that moment needed. Think about it; have you had a good laugh (or laughed at all) in recent times, especially at yourself? If we laughed more, we would undoubtedly stress less and have a better, healthier life.

"A happy heart is good medicine and a joyful mind causes healing, but a broken spirit dries up the bones." Proverbs 17:22 – (AMP).

Go have yourself a dose of some good medicine. It is free, always available and, best of all, you can share it.

W.E.B. Du Bois once said: "I am especially glad of the divine gift of laughter: it has made the world human and lovable, despite all its pain and wrong."

Now go and tear a sock or stocking. Put it on. Go somewhere and have a good laugh. I can tell the medicine is already working. Yes, I see that smile and I hear laughter all around.

LESSON NO. 4

If we use our minds to magnify an ant to the size of an elephant, the reality is, the ant is still as small as it ever was. We often make our fears and other challenges more than they really are and, before we know it, we become stressed out and unhappy.

Blessings And Prayer

Thank you for purchasing this book. My hope and prayer are that in a simple way, it provoked your thoughts and provided for you some inspiration to press through, with a smile and laughter, the various challenges you are facing. I believe our best is never in the past, but it is always before us. Be grateful for what you have and be even more thankful for the people you are blessed to have in your life.

If you have not committed your life to Jesus Christ by accepting Him as your Lord and Saviour, may I encourage you to do so even now. We want all our earthly affairs to be in order, and that I understand. But our eternal soul must also be our priority. Let the words from Paul the Apostle guide you as you make this life changing decision: **"If you openly declare that Jesus is Lord and believe in your heart that God raised him from the dead, you will be saved. For it is by believing in your heart that you are**

made right with God, and it is by openly declaring your faith that you are saved." Romans 10:9-10 – (NLT).

May the Lord Jesus Christ continue to cover, care and comfort you as you put your faith, trust, and hope in Him.

Blessings and peace to you.

About the Author

Howard Anthony Roach accepted Jesus Christ as his personal Saviour and Lord in August 1983. He serves as counsellor, preacher, teacher, worship leader, life coach and mentor. Howard lives by simple principles: much laughter, family, real friends and, every now and then, a bottle of Pepsi. At the epicenter of it all is his relationship with God. Howard believes that every person has within them the potential to achieve great things, no matter where they are from or the support they sometimes lack. He is a graduate of the Jamaica Theological Seminary, ordained minister of Religion, married with two daughters, founding member of Christians Renewed Armed Mission-Driven and Mighty Intl. Ministries.

(C.R.A.M.M.) Howard's Mission is to encourage and challenge people to fulfill their purpose in the earth by becoming who God created them to be.

www.ingramcontent.com/pod-product-compliance
Lightning Source LLC
LaVergne TN
LVHW010514160826
845677LV00012B/2850

* 9 7 9 8 6 6 3 2 7 4 8 4 5 *